BILLS TRACKER

THIS TRACKER
BELONGS TO

....

BILLS TRACKER

DESCRIPTION	DATE	AMOUNT

BILLS TRACKER

DESCRIPTION	DATE	AMOUNT

BILLS TRACKER

DESCRIPTION	DATE	AMOUNT

BILLS TRACKER

DESCRIPTION	DATE	AMOUNT

BILLS TRACKER

DESCRIPTION	DATE	AMOUNT

BILLS TRACKER

DESCRIPTION	DATE	AMOUNT

BILLS TRACKER

DESCRIPTION	DATE	AMOUNT

BILLS TRACKER

DESCRIPTION	DATE	AMOUNT

BILLS TRACKER

DESCRIPTION	DATE	AMOUNT

BILLS TRACKER

DESCRIPTION	DATE	AMOUNT

BILLS TRACKER

DESCRIPTION	DATE	AMOUNT

BILLS TRACKER

DESCRIPTION	DATE	AMOUNT

BILLS TRACKER

DESCRIPTION	DATE	AMOUNT

BILLS TRACKER

DESCRIPTION	DATE	AMOUNT

BILLS TRACKER

DESCRIPTION	*DATE*	*AMOUNT*

BILLS TRACKER

DESCRIPTION	DATE	AMOUNT

BILLS TRACKER

DESCRIPTION	DATE	AMOUNT

BILLS TRACKER

DESCRIPTION	DATE	AMOUNT

BILLS TRACKER

DESCRIPTION	DATE	AMOUNT

BILLS TRACKER

DESCRIPTION	DATE	AMOUNT

BILLS TRACKER

DESCRIPTION	DATE	AMOUNT

BILLS TRACKER

DESCRIPTION	DATE	AMOUNT

BILLS TRACKER

DESCRIPTION	DATE	AMOUNT

BILLS TRACKER

DESCRIPTION	DATE	AMOUNT

BILLS TRACKER

DESCRIPTION	DATE	AMOUNT

BILLS TRACKER

DESCRIPTION	DATE	AMOUNT

BILLS TRACKER

DESCRIPTION	DATE	AMOUNT

BILLS TRACKER

DESCRIPTION	DATE	AMOUNT

BILLS TRACKER

DESCRIPTION	DATE	AMOUNT

BILLS TRACKER

DESCRIPTION	*DATE*	*AMOUNT*

BILLS TRACKER

DESCRIPTION	DATE	AMOUNT

BILLS TRACKER

DESCRIPTION	DATE	AMOUNT

BILLS TRACKER

DESCRIPTION	DATE	AMOUNT

BILLS TRACKER

DESCRIPTION	DATE	AMOUNT

BILLS TRACKER

DESCRIPTION	DATE	AMOUNT

BILLS TRACKER

DESCRIPTION	DATE	AMOUNT

BILLS TRACKER

DESCRIPTION	DATE	AMOUNT

BILLS TRACKER

DESCRIPTION	DATE	AMOUNT

BILLS TRACKER

DESCRIPTION	DATE	AMOUNT

BILLS TRACKER

DESCRIPTION	DATE	AMOUNT

BILLS TRACKER

DESCRIPTION	DATE	AMOUNT

BILLS TRACKER

DESCRIPTION	DATE	AMOUNT

BILLS TRACKER

DESCRIPTION	DATE	AMOUNT

BILLS TRACKER

DESCRIPTION	DATE	AMOUNT

BILLS TRACKER

DESCRIPTION	DATE	AMOUNT

BILLS TRACKER

DESCRIPTION	DATE	AMOUNT

BILLS TRACKER

DESCRIPTION	DATE	AMOUNT

BILLS TRACKER

DESCRIPTION	DATE	AMOUNT

BILLS TRACKER

DESCRIPTION	DATE	AMOUNT

BILLS TRACKER

DESCRIPTION	DATE	AMOUNT

BILLS TRACKER

DESCRIPTION	DATE	AMOUNT

BILLS TRACKER

DESCRIPTION	DATE	AMOUNT

BILLS TRACKER

DESCRIPTION	DATE	AMOUNT

BILLS TRACKER

DESCRIPTION	DATE	AMOUNT

BILLS TRACKER

DESCRIPTION	DATE	AMOUNT

BILLS TRACKER

DESCRIPTION	DATE	AMOUNT

BILLS TRACKER

DESCRIPTION	DATE	AMOUNT

BILLS TRACKER

DESCRIPTION	DATE	AMOUNT

BILLS TRACKER

DESCRIPTION	DATE	AMOUNT

BILLS TRACKER

DESCRIPTION	DATE	AMOUNT

BILLS TRACKER

DESCRIPTION	DATE	AMOUNT

BILLS TRACKER

DESCRIPTION	DATE	AMOUNT

BILLS TRACKER

DESCRIPTION	DATE	AMOUNT

BILLS TRACKER

DESCRIPTION	DATE	AMOUNT

BILLS TRACKER

DESCRIPTION	DATE	AMOUNT

BILLS TRACKER

DESCRIPTION	DATE	AMOUNT

BILLS TRACKER

DESCRIPTION	DATE	AMOUNT

BILLS TRACKER

DESCRIPTION	DATE	AMOUNT

BILLS TRACKER

DESCRIPTION	DATE	AMOUNT

BILLS TRACKER

DESCRIPTION	DATE	AMOUNT

BILLS TRACKER

DESCRIPTION	DATE	AMOUNT

BILLS TRACKER

DESCRIPTION	DATE	AMOUNT

BILLS TRACKER

DESCRIPTION	DATE	AMOUNT

BILLS TRACKER

DESCRIPTION	DATE	AMOUNT

BILLS TRACKER

DESCRIPTION	DATE	AMOUNT

BILLS TRACKER

DESCRIPTION	DATE	AMOUNT

BILLS TRACKER

DESCRIPTION	DATE	AMOUNT

BILLS TRACKER

DESCRIPTION	DATE	AMOUNT

BILLS TRACKER

DESCRIPTION	DATE	AMOUNT

BILLS TRACKER

DESCRIPTION	DATE	AMOUNT

BILLS TRACKER

DESCRIPTION	DATE	AMOUNT

BILLS TRACKER

DESCRIPTION	DATE	AMOUNT

BILLS TRACKER

DESCRIPTION	DATE	AMOUNT

BILLS TRACKER

DESCRIPTION	DATE	AMOUNT

BILLS TRACKER

DESCRIPTION	DATE	AMOUNT

BILLS TRACKER

DESCRIPTION	DATE	AMOUNT

BILLS TRACKER

DESCRIPTION	DATE	AMOUNT

BILLS TRACKER

DESCRIPTION	DATE	AMOUNT

BILLS TRACKER

DESCRIPTION	DATE	AMOUNT

BILLS TRACKER

DESCRIPTION	DATE	AMOUNT

BILLS TRACKER

DESCRIPTION	DATE	AMOUNT

BILLS TRACKER

DESCRIPTION	DATE	AMOUNT

BILLS TRACKER

DESCRIPTION	DATE	AMOUNT

BILLS TRACKER

DESCRIPTION	DATE	AMOUNT

BILLS TRACKER

DESCRIPTION	DATE	AMOUNT

BILLS TRACKER

DESCRIPTION	DATE	AMOUNT

BILLS TRACKER

DESCRIPTION	DATE	AMOUNT

BILLS TRACKER

DESCRIPTION	DATE	AMOUNT

BILLS TRACKER

DESCRIPTION	DATE	AMOUNT

BILLS TRACKER

DESCRIPTION	DATE	AMOUNT

BILLS TRACKER

DESCRIPTION	DATE	AMOUNT

BILLS TRACKER

DESCRIPTION	DATE	AMOUNT

BILLS TRACKER

DESCRIPTION	DATE	AMOUNT

BILLS TRACKER

DESCRIPTION	DATE	AMOUNT

BILLS TRACKER

DESCRIPTION	DATE	AMOUNT

BILLS TRACKER

DESCRIPTION	DATE	AMOUNT

BILLS TRACKER

DESCRIPTION	DATE	AMOUNT

BILLS TRACKER

DESCRIPTION	DATE	AMOUNT

BILLS TRACKER

DESCRIPTION	DATE	AMOUNT

BILLS TRACKER

DESCRIPTION	DATE	AMOUNT

BILLS TRACKER

DESCRIPTION	DATE	AMOUNT

BILLS TRACKER

DESCRIPTION	DATE	AMOUNT

BILLS TRACKER

DESCRIPTION	DATE	AMOUNT

BILLS TRACKER

DESCRIPTION	DATE	AMOUNT

BILLS TRACKER

DESCRIPTION	DATE	AMOUNT

BILLS TRACKER

DESCRIPTION	DATE	AMOUNT

BILLS TRACKER

DESCRIPTION	DATE	AMOUNT

BILLS TRACKER

DESCRIPTION	DATE	AMOUNT

BILLS TRACKER

DESCRIPTION	DATE	AMOUNT

www.ingramcontent.com/pod-product-compliance
Lightning Source LLC
LaVergne TN
LVHW011957070526
838202LV00054B/4947
9786495295268